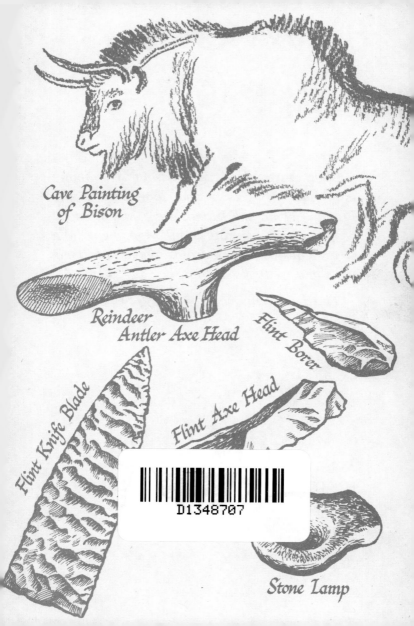

Cave Painting
of Bison

Reindeer
Antler Axe Head

Flint Borer

Flint Knife Blade

Flint Axe Head

Stone Lamp

Series 561

Men have lived in Britain for many thousands of years, and long before the Romans came the islands were inhabited by people whom we call Stone Age men. We give them this name because they made their tools and weapons of flint.

This book tells you something of how they lived.

A LADYBIRD
HISTORY
BOOK

2'6
NET

AN ADVENTURE FROM HISTORY

STONE AGE MAN
IN BRITAIN

by
L. DU GARDE PEACH

with illustrations by
JOHN KENNEY

Publishers: Wills & Hepworth Ltd., Loughborough

First published 1961   ©   *Printed in England*

STONE AGE MAN IN BRITAIN

The British Isles were not always the green and pleasant land in which we live to-day. Many thousands of years ago they were not even islands. The Straits of Dover did not exist, and England was joined to France by dry land.

In those far off times no one lived here because the land was covered with ice hundreds of feet thick. Where there are now valleys, were what are called glaciers: great rivers of ice slowly moving down hill to the sea.

These glaciers weighed millions of tons, and as they moved, they scraped away the rocky sides of the hills. This is how many of the valleys in the British Isles were formed.

Then slowly the climate became warmer and the ice melted, leaving the bare rock underneath. There were no trees or flowers, and many hundreds of years passed before the land was fit for men to live in.

Even before the trees and grass began to grow in Britain, the earliest men ever to live here came across the dry land from France.

These men and women were very different from the men and women of to-day. If we could see them, we should probably think that they were not human beings at all, because they were covered with hair and had fierce animal-like faces.

We should be wrong. These men of thousands of years ago were able to talk and think, though only in a very simple way. They knew how to make some sort of clothes for themselves out of the skins of animals, and they lived together in little family groups.

They had not yet learned how to build even the simplest houses, and in winter they must have been very uncomfortable, as well as being constantly in danger from wild beasts.

Near Torquay, in Devon, there is a cave called Kent's Cavern. This is one of the caves in which these men lived, more than ten thousand years ago.

There are many of these caves in England and in countries on the Continent. We know that these people lived in them, because buried in the clay or soil of the floors we find the charred bones of the animals which they hunted for food.

On the rocky walls of some of these caves in France, there are drawings of horses and deer and other animals. These are amazingly well done, and show the sort of animals which were living at that time.

Writing had not been invented in those days, but from these pictures and such stone tools as have been found in the caves, we can get some idea of the way these people lived, long before the dawn of history.

These men and women are our ancestors, and it is interesting to all of us to know something about their daily lives.

Perhaps the most important thing about them is that they knew how to make fire, probably by rubbing very dry sticks together. This made a great difference to their lives, because it meant that they could cook their food.

They had, of course, no iron or steel knives, or anything at all made of metal. Their spears and cutting tools were made of flint, which they chipped to a sharp edge and used for all purposes.

Nor had they any pottery, because they had not found out how to model clay and harden it in a fire.

We must think of these animal-like people as having none of the things which we use every day of our lives.

There are no dangerous wild animals in Britain to-day, but when these people lived here they had very often to hide from the many savage beasts which roamed the country.

Amongst these were huge animals which no longer exist anywhere on the earth, such as the mammoth. This was an animal larger than an elephant, and which was very dangerous.

Other wild and dangerous animals were savage sabre-toothed tigers and cave bears, as well as the woolly rhinoceros—animals which have now entirely disappeared.

These animals were hunted with flint weapons and with a thing called a bolas. This was a long cord made of skin or sinews, with a stone at each end. When it was thrown at an animal, it wrapped round the animal's legs so that it fell down. It could then be killed with a flint spear.

About six or seven thousand years ago, some new people came across the dry land into England. We call them the Neolithic people, and we know that they were much more intelligent than the men who lived in caves.

These new people were still dressed in the skins of animals, but they had found out how to make bows and arrows. This meant that they could hunt the wild animals with far less danger to themselves, because they could shoot them from a distance with their arrows.

One of the main reasons why men are different from animals is that men have brains which can think and remember. The cave man's brain was undeveloped, and he did not think very much. The Neolithic men had better brains, and when they saw things happening they wanted to know why they happened. This desire to find out why things happened was the beginning of all civilisation.

Let us look for a moment at the kind of country which these new people found when they crossed from France over the dry land, which in those days joined France and England.

There were, of course, no roads or houses, and no fields or hedges. Instead of these things, the newcomers found forests and swamps in the valleys, and chalk uplands or heather-covered hills.

If you look at what is called a contour map of the British Isles, you will see where the hills are situated. It was on these that Neolithic men and women mostly lived.

There was a good reason for this. They had no steel axes with which to cut down the trees of the forests, and even if they had been able to do so, they could not have drained the swampy land on which the forests grew. To live on the dry chalk hills, like the South Downs, was much easier for them, and it is here that we find the remains which tell us all we know about them.

We do not know what language these people spoke, or what sort of names they had for one another. If a man could run very fast they probably called him Quick Foot, of course in their own language. Let us see how he lived.

Quick Foot was not satisfied to live in a cave, like the people who came when the ice disappeared. He wanted to live on the dry, chalky soil of the South Downs, so he had to think about making a house or hut for himself and his family.

First he dug a hole in the ground, about two feet deep, and piled stones and turf round the edge until there was a wall four or five feet high. Across the top he put branches of trees and covered them with grass and reeds, with a layer of turf or skins on top.

It was not a very comfortable house, but Quick Foot was very proud of it. It kept out the rain and the snow, and it was certainly warmer than a cave.

Now that Quick Foot had a hut, he could think about making flint knives and arrow-heads, with which to go hunting.

In order to do this, he looked about for a large piece of flint, a shiny sort of stone which splits up into sharp flakes. When he found one, he hammered it with another stone until he had got a lot of sharp-edged pieces.

He next looked the pieces over very carefully. Some of them were no use at all, but some were long and thin, and very nearly the right shape for knives or arrow-heads.

Quick Foot had plenty of time and a lot of patience, and all day long he sat carefully chipping at the little flakes of flint and rubbing them on hard rocks, until they were beautifully shaped arrow-heads, or thin sharp knives with which to skin the animals he killed.

Besides hunting animals for food, these Neolithic men used their skins to make clothes for themselves and their wives and children.

The people who had lived in caves used the skins just as they were, but this was not good enough for the men who came after them. They cut the skins to the right shape with flint knives, and fastened the pieces together to make better fitting clothes.

It took these people a long time to think out how to make what we call a needle and thread. Even then it was only a thin piece of bone with a hole through one end, and some lengths of sinew.

Now they could sew the pieces of skin together and make quite warm, fur-lined clothes. What was more, they were very practical clothes: they kept out the rain and did not wear out.

The rivers of England were full of fish in those days, as they still are to-day, and sometimes men like Quick Foot would lie on the river bank and try to catch them in their hands.

This is very difficult, because fish are too slippery to hold, and they move very quickly. So these early fishermen tried hard to think of a better way of catching them.

Perhaps one day one of them was sewing some skins together, but at the back of his mind he was still trying to think of a good way to catch fish.

It could have been the bone needle which gave him the idea. "If I made a bone needle with a little hook on the end," he may have thought, "and then got a fish to swallow it, I could pull it out of the river."

So he scraped away at a little bone with his flint knife, and soon he had a fish-hook with which to go fishing in the rivers.

These men of long ago were now able to go hunting and fishing, and to sit around the fire in their huts when it was cold and wet outside.

But they wanted to travel further afield, and in a land of rivers and lakes they needed something in which to cross the water. So after a lot of thinking about it, they made a dug-out canoe.

Of course they had never seen one, but they had tried to sit on tree trunks floating in the water. These always rolled over, and they thought that if they could sit *in* the tree trunk, instead of *on* it, it would remain steady.

To hollow out a tree trunk with a flint knife was very difficult, but charred wood is much easier to scrape away. So they lit fires along the tree trunk and scraped away the charred wood as the fire burned down.

In this way they made canoes in which they could cross the lakes and rivers.

The people who had lived in caves had used tame dogs for hunting, but they had no other animals.

When the new people came across from France they brought with them some sheep, goats, pigs and small black cows. So instead of having to hunt for all their food, they had pigs for bacon and cattle for beef on the spot.

These people were farmers—very simple farmers—but the first of the millions of farmers who have lived on the soil of England ever since.

Up to this time no man had ever tasted anything like bread. Everybody had lived on meat of one sort or another, and the fruit and berries which they found growing wild.

The next step was to grow some sort of corn out of which to make bread.

We do not know how these people who lived here in Britain so long ago, first came to grow corn.

Perhaps Quick Foot's wife, or some other woman, threw away some grass seeds beside the hut and noticed that they grew. Then she may have planted some more, and when these grew, cooked them in milk from the cows or goats, and made a sort of porridge.

But the seeds became dry and hard, and perhaps she thought that if she rubbed them between two stones, they would make better porridge. To her surprise, they made something quite different.

By crushing the seeds she had made a rough sort of flour, and when it was cooked with water or milk, it became bread.

Everybody liked the new sort of food, so they planted more seeds, and made shallow holes in flat stones, with other stones fitting into them, to grind the seeds into flour.

People in Britain were now becoming more and more domesticated.

This means that instead of being wandering savages, they were living in villages of huts like the one Quick Foot had built, and working their little farms.

About this time another great advance was made towards better living conditions. The Stone Age men discovered how to make pottery.

Clay was abundant, and it was noticed that when it was shaped and exposed to the fire, it became hard and, what was more important, capable of keeping its shape and holding water.

Bowls and dishes made by these early people have been found. They were roughly shaped by hand and without the shiny glazed surface which our cups and saucers have to-day. But the most interesting thing about them is that the bowls all have a round or pointed base. This means that they were not intended to stand on a table. It is probable that they were propped up by stones, and that a fire was built round them to heat whatever they contained.

By this time men had discovered a new way of lighting a fire.

The cave men had rubbed dry sticks together, but this is a very slow and difficult way of making fire. One day one of the Neolithic men may have been chipping away at a flint to make a knife, and the sparks which always fly when flint is chipped may have fallen on some dry moss. Immediately the moss would have begun to smoulder, and when the man blew on it, it burst into flames.

Ever after that he and the other men carried pieces of flint and some dry moss about with them, so that they could easily light a fire whenever they wanted to.

It is interesting to remember that this way of making fire was still used until just over a hundred years ago, when matches were invented. Even to-day, a petrol lighter makes a spark in the same way, to set fire to the wick.

The huts built in the early days did not stand all alone on the South Downs. A lot of other men like Quick Foot had built huts just like his all around him. Probably a hundred families lived close together in a little village of huts, with a wall round it to keep out wild animals.

These little villages must always have had some man who was stronger or wiser than the others, and soon such a man might become the chief of a whole tribe living in different villages all over the Downs.

There were no roads or even footpaths in Britain when the cave men lived here, but now the people of one village often went to the other villages to exchange corn for fish or to bargain for flint tools.

On these journeys they always went by the easiest way, and soon beaten tracks were made through the woods or across the hills from one village to another.

These were the beginnings of the roads of Britain to-day.

There came a day when the men of another tribe thought that instead of raising their own cattle, it would be easier to steal the cows and sheep belonging to some nearby tribe.

So they came over the hills with their flint spears and their bows and arrows, and there was a fierce battle before they were beaten off.

Then all the men of the tribe got together and decided to make a strong fortress where they would be safe from attack.

They had no tools with which to build a stone castle, but they had bone shovels made from the shoulder blades of the deer which they hunted for food.

With these they dug a deep ditch, piling up the earth behind it, around the top of a hill. Many of these hill-top forts can still be seen in Britain.

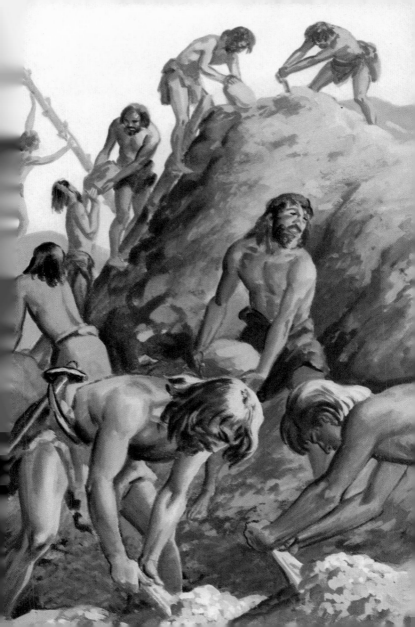

When a leader died, the whole tribe gathered together to make a tomb worthy of their chief.

By piling together a number of heavy stones they built a sort of stone hut, roofed over with larger flat slabs of rock. Inside it, with the body of their chief, they left his flint weapons and ornaments.

Then over the stone hut they raised a great mound of earth. Many of these burial mounds still exist in Britain.

There were in those days no churches, because these people worshipped the sun. They realized that without it, life could not exist, so they built great circles and avenues of stone at places where, at certain times of the year, they came for their religious festivals.

Things did not change quickly in those days, and even a thousand years after Quick Foot died, the people were still living in the same kind of huts, using the same sort of flint knives, and sewing the skins of animals together for clothes.

But they had learned how to shape great blocks of stone by hammering them with other stones, and the bowls which they made were decorated with patterns cut in the wet clay before they were hardened in the fire.

About two-thousand years before the birth of Christ, there must have been some wise and powerful man who was the chief of a great many tribes and villages in the south of England.

He and the chief men of all the tribes decided to build a great temple for the sun god.

The temple which they built still stands on Salisbury Plain in Wiltshire. It is called Stonehenge.

The work of building Stonehenge must have employed many hundreds of men, because the great stones were brought from many miles away. Some of them came from quarries in Wales, a distance of 150 miles from where they now stand.

Even to-day, with cranes and ships and railways, it would be quite a difficult task to bring these great stones, some of which weighed nearly thirty tons, from Pembroke-shire to Salisbury Plain.

We know the quarries from which the stones came, but we can only guess how these people quarried them, nearly four-thousand years ago.

Probably they drove wooden pegs into cracks in the cliffs and then poured water on them. As the wet wood expanded, it split great pieces of stone away from the cliffs' sides.

The stones had now to be shaped. This was done by hammering them with other stones. Hundreds of men must have been busy for many months, slowly flattening out the rough surfaces and shaping the corners.

The leading men of the tribes were very busy all this time arranging how the stones were to be brought across rough country to Wiltshire.

They may have come by way of where Gloucester stands to-day. Strong tree trunks would be used as levers to lift one end at a time, whilst other tree trunks were placed under them as rollers. Then hundreds of men would haul the stones along, a few yards at a time, pulling on ropes made of plaited leather.

Or they may have been levered on to large rafts and floated along the Bristol Channel, and up the River Avon to some-where near Bath.

All this must have taken years, but at last they were ready for setting up.

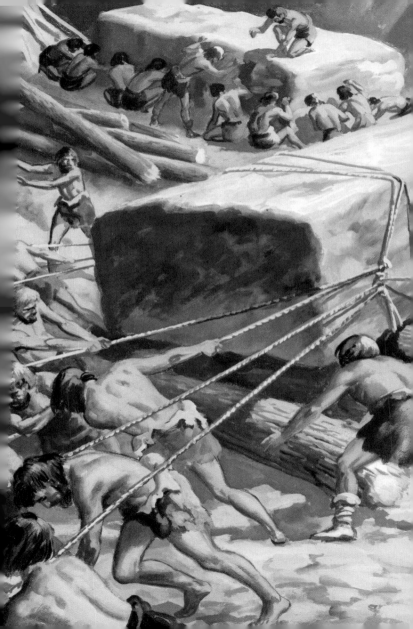

These early builders now had to think out some way of making the stones stand upright.

Quite recently some of these stones which had fallen down, have been lifted upright by powerful cranes. Even so, it was very difficult and took a long time.

The man who ordered the building of Stonehenge had no cranes. But he had thousands of men to work for him, so he made them start by digging a hole for each stone to stand in. Then the men piled up a sloping mound of earth with a straight up and down end at the edge of the hole.

The stone was next hauled up the slope on rollers until it overbalanced and one end fell into the hole. The mound of earth was then removed and the hole filled up round the stone.

Many of the stones still stand where they were first set up. They have not moved an inch in four-thousand years.

So, you see, although they could not write their story in words for us to read, we know quite a lot about these men who lived in Britain so long ago.

How do we know all this?

It is by the patient work of men and women who dig in the ground in places where Neolithic men lived, and who find the flint tools which they used and the simple articles of bone and pottery which they made.

To-day we should call these early inhabitants of Britain savages. But although the Stone Age men were a very primitive race, every now and then there would be amongst them some man like Quick Foot who could think better than the others. Then some small advance would be made— like the discovery of pottery or the use of the roller and lever.

They were not savages. They were the dim beginnings of the modern civilisation in which you and all of us now live.

Arrow Heads

Hand Axe

Spearhead

Cooking Pot

Bone Needles

Cutting Tool

Cave Painting of Horse

Bone Harpoon